I0468849

SOCIAL MEDIA

How to Turn the Market Upside Down by Using Marketing Strategies on Social Network

By JOSHUA ELANS

Table of Contents

Introduction

Social media has truly revolutionized the world of marketing. With advances in technology, namely, the advent of the Internet, the marketing paradigm has seen a shift to where now, one the most effective ways to generate awareness is leveraging social media. Unlike traditional marketing channels, the startup costs to leveraging the social media platform are extremely low and in many instances, free. However, the reach of social media is astronomical. Just ask the video blogger who has gained national notoriety through a YouTube channel or the millionaire whose net worth was built off videos posted through the same channel, the return on investment when leveraging social media is nothing short of astonishing.

Social Media is a powerful marketing tool and the potential results may be life altering. Yet in still, most people do not experience the fullness of what social media has to offer. In order to optimize results for this platform – having a strategy is a must. A strategy is a plan of action, one that consists of goals and objectives, outlining exactly what outcome one is seeking in leveraging a social media channel. There must be a brand voice, and that voice needs to connect and engage with a target audience that is strategically selected to help move marketing goals into successes. Having an intimate knowledge of the widely used social media platforms and selecting ones that will have the most impact in connecting with the target audience is required. Time spent developing engaging content lies as one of the cornerstones of an effective social media strategy. Finally, continuously reviewing and refreshing this plan to ensure it continues to align with goals; these all play a factor in developing an effective strategy that would enable an individual to get the very most out of social media.

Creating a powerful strategy is not impossible to do. It takes research, time, dedication and perseverance to see results. Social media holds more than enough potential to allow an individual to shake up any market and take the world by storm – a person needs to be able to unlock the marketing power of social media by familiarizing oneself with the steps necessary to develop an effective social media strategy.

Chapter 1: The World of Social Media and Influence

Social media and the different platforms that encompass this phenomenon have literally, "taken the world by storm." To say social media's reach may be certainly branded as an understatement of epic proportions; Social Media has managed to touch the lives of every single person within age and knowledge of how to use a computer, smartphone or tablet. If you look around – one will be hard pressed to find anyone who does not use at least one form of Social Media platform for one purpose or another.

Social Media is primarily a tool of engagement; one serving several purposes and filling many needs. It is a powerful marketing tool; one that can take an invention, concept or even a persona and launch it into a universal awareness.

This medium can and has spurred movements, highlighting critical issues that call for both an attentiveness and as well as a responsiveness. It is an instrument that helps us to come together, connect and reconnect: allowing us a look into each another's lives that we most likely would not be privy to without the availability of platforms such as Facebook or

Instagram. In times of social or political unrest, social media acts as the voice of the people.

Therefore, it is of utmost importance, in this age where awareness comes in the digital archetype known as social media, that we as individuals must understand how to leverage this tool, in order to fill everyone's unique needs and purposes. Again, social media is a very powerful instrument – one that is at the disposal of many – but unfortunately, used to its fullest potential by very few. Social media is transformative. It has the ability to take any kind of project and taking it to an exponentially higher level of awareness. Developing a strategy, that is, creating a plan that optimizes the use of social media is key to unlocking its great and many benefits. Whatever the market is; strategically using this platform would allow anyone to shake things up; virtually turning any market upside down!

Chapter 2: Titans of Social Media Platforms

An Introduction to the Principal Social Media Channels

In this age of social media, there are several different platforms. These types target every kind of niche market one can imagine. From those who choose to tell their narrative through photography or others who simply want to stay connected through professional networks; there is a social media outlet there to connect every kind of group imaginable.

Among these, however, there are four outlets that are widely known and utilized. These may be known as the leaders, if you will, of social media. These vehicles are ones that will generate a significant amount of traffic, and traffic itself is a key indicator of a solid social media strategy. If an individual is going to leverage social media to create awareness of a new product, a blog or a talent, then having a place within one of these mediums is a must. Again, since these are the most widely used; this means the potential number of connections a person can make is a lot higher than opting for a lesser known and marginally used social media platform. These social networking services are known as Facebook, Twitter, YouTube and Instagram.

FACEBOOK

Facebook is a social media website that allows you to connect with family and friends. Facebook fosters a community of users. Through these connections, which are referred to as "friends," a person is able to share a host of special moments with others who are included in the circle of friends. From photos to videos – a person is able to post virtually any content to their timeline and the Facebook algorithm allows it so that feedback – at any length - is accepted on each post. An individual can "like" a photo and or provide written responses in the form of comments.

Facebook leverages relationships in degrees. This means, if John Smith is friends with Mary Brown, and Mary Brown is James Green's friend, then Facebook will make the suggestion to John Smith that he should send a friend request to James Green. A person's Facebook network of family and friends is able to grow exponentially through using second, third and even fourth-degree relationships.

There is also a fan page component to Facebook. These pages bring a group together, not based on familial or friendship ties, but around a particular product or interest. It takes marketing efforts to build a network on a fan page.

Three years back, Facebook was cited as the most widely used with an estimated 1.15 billion monthly active users. That number is substantially larger today

YOUTUBE

YouTube is a video sharing platform. Videos are shared and feedback is available through a thumbs up or a thumbs down. Comments may also be left in reaction to posted videos.

Unlike Facebook, YouTube's network is not dependent on connections. People simply opt to follow a particular "YouTubers" page, which is known as a channel. A person looking to increase their number of followers, or grow their channel, must actively market and recruit followers. Usually, another social media platform is used as the marketing tool to generate awareness around an individual's YouTube channel. YouTube differs from a lot of other mediums in that you are actually able to monetize the videos posted; thereby earning money each time a video is viewed.

A great portion of the popularity of this social media website stems from YouTube being the "go to" of social media when a person needs to learn a skill for free, quickly and efficiently. From learning how to change a bit from an electric drill to baking the perfect chocolate chip cookie, YouTube is packed with a number of video tutorials. YouTube is also a good option for finding entertaining personalities; ones who upload a variety of videos - from discussing and recapping currently airing television shows to simply fan pages dedicated to singers; there really is content for anyone on YouTube.

As far as the size of this platform – YouTube was identified as being closely behind Facebook with 1 billion monthly active users.

TWITTER

Twitter is a social media website that allows you to follow others as well as in turn, is followed. Twitter is unique in that feedback doesn't play a central role as it would in either Facebook or YouTube. Instead, quick status updates are allowed, ones with a 140 character limit – just enough to quickly convey a thought or feeling. This series of updates are known as "tweets."

Twitter stands apart from Facebook and YouTube in that on Twitter, a person has the ability to be followed by several thousand people. For instance, to have 10,000 friends on

Facebook would mean that it is highly likely that a person has some level of notoriety; 10,000 friends is not easily attained. On Twitter, getting 10,000 followers, with the right strategy, is something easier accomplished than on other social media sites.

Twitter also stands apart in that it provides the individual with celebrity access. A connection is easier made to those of influence and fame than with other platforms. A tweet is easier liked, retweeted and responded to by a celebrity, than by commenting under a star's photo on Facebook. Speaking from my own experience, I have been afforded the opportunity to trade quick tweets with several celebrities on Twitter. However, on Facebook, I've never received a celebrity acknowledgment to any of my celebrity targeted comments.

While not as large as Facebook and YouTube, Twitter is still highly recognized as a leading social media site. When brands or companies are making a request to connect – Twitter is always presented as one of the options for making that connection.

INSTAGRAM

Finally, Instagram rounds out the most highly recognizable of social media platforms. Instagram is primarily a photo sharing platform. While videos may be uploaded as well; the length of these are 15 seconds or less. Instagram allows a person to tell their narrative through photos. Instagram followers are recommended through Facebook connections. From there an individual may follow others based on common interests and in turn, may be followed as well. Like Twitter, while not boasting the monthly active users as Facebook or YouTube, Instagram remains as one of the most recognizable of social media platforms.

Chapter 3: Understand the Audience

While social media is a powerful marketing tool with the potential to produce great success; attaining the results one seeks is by no means instantaneous. Creating a viable social media strategy takes time and research. One of the initial questions a person needs to ask themselves before putting forth any kind of effort in crafting a social media plan is: Who is my audience? Again, social media is the instrument that allows for a brand to reach a wide audience, however, if the individual is unaware of who this targeted group of people that needs to be reached are – the power that social media has is nullified. In short, an effective marketing plan targets an audience and uses the social media platform to speak to that specific group.

An individual may take a few different approaches in seeking to understand their audience. Primarily, one must understand what the demographic of the audience, in fact, consists of. Are the members female or male? What is the age group of the target? What are some of the occupations members of this audience may be employed? Secondary questions to consider would be what drives or motivates the target audience member? Why is this group using social media? More importantly, which social media channels are they using?

Another approach one could take is creating different personas for the audience. Creating different personalities would answer many of the questions a person would need to know in figuring out the types of people they seek to target. The persona created would help tell a story about the audience and, therefore, help the marketer to understand the several different approaches that may be leveraged in communicating with this particular group through social media.

The purpose of understanding the audience is to ensure the right messages are getting to the right people. There needs to be much time taken in this step and it certainly should not be rushed. Understanding the audience and how to engage with them surely acts as one of the cornerstones to an effective social media strategy – one that can move any marketplace!

Chapter 4: Develop a Brand Voice

Once an individual has determined the social media engine that will be employed, now is the time to create a brand voice with which to speak on your selected platform. For example, if a person is creating a social media strategy to bring awareness to a new online store; then what "personality" would the store have? What kind of relationship would a person look towards fostering between the store and the target audience? Developing a brand voice is what will drive the way in which social media is employed; the brand voice, when created strategically, aids in the receptivity of your message to your audience.

Again, the brand voice dictates the content of the chosen social media platforms. The tone of the communications of Facebook posts, the look of a YouTube channel; these are all influenced by the brand voice. It is important for the voice of the brand to be impactful, engaging and most importantly, consistent. Since a major part of social media strategy focuses on making connections with a target audience; your brand voice and social media platform must work cohesively in generating the results being sought from marketing objectives created.

The brand voice is an important element to effectively leveraging social media and creating a solid brand strategy. As such, this part of the strategy should be one that is carefully crafted. A good exercise in developing a brand voice is to simply compile a list of adjectives of what the brand being promoted is. Looking at these adjectives would allow an individual to begin to craft a brand identity and a voice to use through social media.

Let's take an example from Rebecca's Nail Art blog. After careful thought, Rebecca opted to choose a "nail design project paradise" brand voice. Rebecca decides that her brand voice is cheerful and upbeat, therefore, she opts to bring her brand voice to life with a vibrant plum and hot pink color scheme. Rebecca uses cheerful, lively terminology in her Facebook posts. Her Twitter page header is designed with the plum and pink color scheme. Finally, Rebecca is sure to use high-energy and vivacious words in the YouTube videos that she creates of her nail design projects.

Carefully developing a brand voice and strategically incorporating it into your social media plan will bring your project, product or persona into another dimension of awareness. Turning the market upside down with social media means carefully crafting a relatable voice that tactically reaches the intended audience.

Chapter 5: Establish Social Media Goals

Setting Objectives

No matter what the platform, social media a powerful marketing tool. The key to being able to draw out the key benefits of social media lies in knowing what your goals for using this medium in fact are. In other words: in order to develop an effective social media strategy, first an individual must establish a clear objective; and from there be able to measure progress against goals.

What are a person's goals? This requires some thought as a clear and streamlined objective will later prove to be the cornerstone of an impactful social media strategy. Is an individual creating awareness for a new product? Is a person looking to create passive income by creating and growing a YouTube channel? Is there a blog that needs more traffic? An individual would need to effectively assess where they are aiming for social media to take them; a goal needs to be specific to the need of the marketer.

Examples of objectives pertinent to social media and optimizing it use include:

- Creating product or brand awareness
- Generating Income
- Establishing a brand identity
- Converting followers

When setting objectives, simple always works best. With the varied directions, one can go in social media marketing, there is the temptation to set multiple goals. The best course of action would be to set one goal and create a strategy centered on that one or at the most two, objectives. This way, a person's efforts are streamlined for optimal results.

Measure Your Goals

Goal measurement is an absolute necessity in setting objectives that are part of the strategy. Without a baseline of which to measure objectives against – the effectiveness of a plan cannot be ascertained. These measurements should be clear and easily observed. For instance, an individual looking to grow views per month to a blog would set a goal that looks for a percentage increase to views within a specified time period. Someone looking to generate revenue from a new product would set a goal that tracks website visits that convert into sales. In short, once an objective is set, there should be a way to quantify progress. While an effective social media strategy calls for setting one objective; the measurement of this objective should be more than one and should work in tandem with one another in helping to reach your established objectives.

Chapter 6: Select a Platform

Once an individual is able to ascertain what their goals are for leveraging social media, what should follow is choosing a platform that will optimize results. While taking a cross-platform approach is beneficial, it is important to understand that having an effective strategy in place calls for choosing a primary social media outlet that will provide the best results. Certain goals are better met by using one social networking site over another, as the closer your social media vehicle is aligned to your objectives – one is able to create strategic content to help achieve marketing objectives.

To begin, brainstorming should be the first activity at hand. The questions that should be focused on include: Who is the target audience? Once a target is identified, what follows should be: What is the best way to reach the target audience through social media? Reaching an audience means building personal connections. If used correctly, social media has the ability to make a powerful impact in giving an individual a voice and, in turn, a connection, with the target group at hand.

Rebecca Smith's Nail Art Blog

In order to illustrate, let's take another look at Rebecca Smith's Nail Art blog. The goal for Rebecca's blog is to be one that is revenue generating. Therefore, the marketing objective she will be employing is to increase monthly views to her blog incrementally over the next six month period. Rebecca's goal is established – now is the time for her to strategically pick the social media platform that will deliver the best results against this objective.

After some research, Rebecca Smith determines that her target audience for nail art and design are women who are mainly between the ages of 25 to 40 years old. Rebecca goes even further and creates a persona of her target audience – What inspires the woman who loves nail designs? What are the important aspects of nail art – aspects that would allow the woman to reach out and seek answers from a social media outlet? What information can she offer that would foster a connection between Rebecca Smith and her target audience? Rebecca is able to determine that acquiring new nail art project ideas, nail design patterns and finding beautiful and unique new shades of nail polish, are what motivates the woman who loves nail art. From there, Rebecca strategically creates engaging content based on a nail art lover's topics of main interest. What Rebecca now needs to determine is which social media vehicle will be most effective in maximizing the number in her target she desires to reach.

This is where knowledge of the different social media platforms are of utmost importance. Understanding how these mediums are used as well as the nuances that exist between them are key to understanding how to strategically leverage different social media types.

Nail art projects would call for a visual medium; one that allows a "how to" narrative to be told primarily through images. Twitter would not be as effective as while you are able to post photos on Twitter, an individual would not be able to walk through a nail art project using this platform. Rebecca narrows her choices down to YouTube, as she can easily create an engaging nail project and then upload the videos for others to see and attempt for themselves; or Pinterest, where she can take an impactful photo of the end result of the project – a hand of beautifully manicured nails, add it to her nail art board and then create a link to her blog for those who want to try the project. In the end, Rebecca chooses to lead with Pinterest because it closely ties back to her main objective of increasing website views to her blog. However, she also opts to upload a video on YouTube as a how to and will also use twitter as a secondary vehicle to create a quick awareness around her blog and video.

Choosing a platform that optimizes your efforts to connect with others and being consistent with the chosen strategy will create successful results that will allow an individual to be a real force to contend with in his or her respective market.

Chapter 7: Developing Content

Engage, Engage & Engage!

Creating engaging content simply means creating something; whether it is a Facebook post, YouTube video or Pinterest pin, that draws a response and opens the conversation between the marketer and members of the target audience. Engaging content can take a brand to new, soaring heights, whereas lack of engaging material can leave an individual marketing a brand feeling discouraged and frustrated at the lack of response. Optimizing social media as a marketing tool means making every effort produce content that is closely aligned with the interests of the target audience. Content that is compelling invokes a response that provides an opportunity to connect.

The heart of an effective plan lies in the ability to reach a target audience and compel the group with meaningful, entertaining and interesting subject matter. In fact, the bulk of time spent on creating an effective strategy will be in developing engaging content to disseminate through different social media channels.

Creating content can be very challenging, especially since most people are not content marketers. However, through practice and trial and error, assessing what type of content garners more engagement than others, one is able to create a baseline for what works. Some ideas for creating content include researching industry trends and presenting these to the audience in an entertaining way. Sharing personal stories (both successes and opportunities) with tips and tricks related to the market. Using media outlets such as the news can assist with creating material as highlighting a news headline as a Facebook post and asking a question is a good way to open the conversation with an audience. Creating how-to guides are always a good choice for producing interesting content.

Minimize content that works towards selling a product or service. These may be construed as "spam" techniques and in turn, can hurt in efforts to connect with the target audience. In general, people do not trust someone who is always trying to "make the sale." Instead, 90% of the content should include topics that are of interest to the particular group.

Looking at Rebecca Smith's nail blog, Rebecca creates engaging content in a few different ways. Rebecca interviews her own manicurist, who happens to be the top nail designer in her neighborhood, and she uploads this video to her YouTube channel. Rebecca leverages Pinterest to upload photos featuring manicured hands with seasonal trends in nail polish colors. Finally, Rebecca creates weekly how-to blog posts that feature easy-to-do, beautiful nail designs and creates awareness of these posts using Facebook.

Optimizing Content

Once content is created – one should optimize content for best results. Being sure to take steps in doing so will ensure the subject matter is as far-reaching as possible. Ideas for enhancing content include using attention-grabbing headlines – making sure the first few words are persuasive enough to immediately capture the focus of someone skimming through a social media medium. Understanding and utilizing search engine optimization is very important, in order to ensure the right people are being steered to the content. Finally, including compelling images or photos to create an interesting environment, one that visually makes the audience member want to continue to read through the subject matter.

Consistency

The key to success in leveraging social media includes being consistent. One Facebook post every month will not yield successful results. A weekly Facebook post, one added consistently over a long period of time will most certainly produce the results that will positively impact an individual's marketing objectives. In order to reach a broader audience and experience the transformative power of social media, content must be consistently created and dispersed through the selected channel. An easy way to ensure consistent content is to dedicate a few hours a week creating the content and then automating posts. A good example would be Facebook, an individual is able to create a post and create a schedule, specifying when the content is to be displayed.

Chapter 8: Social Media Channel Plans

Once there is an understanding of why social media will be used to target a specific audience; there must be a strategic social media channel plan in place to execute against. A social media channel plan is one that specifies the "what's" and the "when's" each medium will take. A channel plan is comprehensive, it serves as the complete guide detailing all of the tactical elements that will come together in order to optimize the strength of each platform. This plan takes a schedule of content and timing of releasing the content and puts it into an easy to access design. It makes the marketer aware of what content needs to be shared, and when, for each social media platform. Creating a social media channel plan does involve some time and a few steps.

Channel Objectives

If Facebook is the lead channel driving strategy, one should start there. From there, an individual should create objectives specific to the channel. Is the Facebook objective an increase of follower engagement measured by an upsurge of likes per post? Or is the goal higher conversion marked by new followers? Understand and establish what each channel's goals are in helping to build a social media channel strategy.

Content Strategy

The content strategy delineates the narrative being told, it creates a framework for the story. The content strategy drives how the story is going to be told through the respective channel. Taking, for instance, the goal to increase Facebook engagement by an upsurge of likes. Since Facebook is a channel whose main premise focuses on the community; creating a post that allows for the voice of a group to be heard would be what drives the content selected.

For Rebecca Smith's nail blog, an example of her creating this kind of content would be to create a series of polling Facebook posts. Rebecca would post photos of intricate, Avant–Garden all designs and ask for a vote of yay or nay. The voting opens up a stream of feedback from the audience member and encourages dialogue. In the grander scheme, it also encourages and reinforces the community between nail design lovers.

Editorial Plan

An editorial plan is simply the schedule created that dictates what content will be posted and the elected time of posting. Additionally, the editorial plan outlines how often content is submitted through the chosen channel, the tone that will be used through the medium and it also defines what the desired action for the audience reading the content is.

Chapter 9: Gather Competitive Intelligence

Competitive intelligence simply refers to what the competition is doing. In the landscape of social media strategy, gathering intelligence is conducting research into the different social media channels out there to see how these are leveraged by competitors in a similar marketplace.

In attending trade shows as a former marketing manager, one of my primary responsibilities included gathering competitive. This duty entailed inconspicuously walking a trade show floor to see anything new from the competition, observe how they leveraged booth space at a show and see if there were many people there, waiting to speak with the competitor. During one of these shows, I was talking to a competitor and I came to the sudden realization that I had the logo of the company I was employed by imprinted on the upper left corner of my shirt. Trying to save face, I tried to cover it with my hand (visualize me suddenly standing in a pledge of allegiance stance), but by then I was caught. The conversation ended abruptly; the competitor thanking me for my time and moving on to speak with someone else.

Thankfully, social media is a digital medium! This wouldn't be the case for the marketer who is attempting to gather competitive online. It is relatively easy to view the competition and see how they are leveraging the different social media channels without leaving the obvious footprint that I did during my one encounter.

One of the most powerful reasons for gathering this kind of intelligence is to observe the tools of engagement being used channel wide to draw the attention of the target audience. If a competitor utilizes YouTube and has 25,000 followers on their page, chances are they have an effective strategy in place to draw these kinds of numbers. This is not to say one should steal or replicate content from a competitor; as such as an action, at its core, is unscrupulous. However, getting an idea of what an audience responds to from those in a similar marketplace will only help an individual in creating a solid social media strategy.

Chapter 10: Time, Dedication & Perseverance

If one were to choose the most important factors in creating a solid social media strategy, it would undeniably be time, dedication and persevering with the plan. A marketer may have a powerful strategy in place, one that will leave not one persona or target audience untouched, however, if there isn't the dedication there; it really is all for naught. A person must spend the time continuously executing against the strategy. There must be the dedication to constantly review the social media plan and refresh goals, objectives and tactics as needed. There must be an innate perseverance present within the individual to continue against all the ebbs and flows one may find in the digital world of the social media.

As a marketing tool, social media has revolutionized the way people are reached and connections are made. Social media's ultimate influence, being, the ability to make people aware, can have life-changing results. However, if time is not spent cultivating an effective plan of engagement, and executing against that plan, then the power of social media is never truly unlocked – it's great potential never to be experienced.

Time, dedication and perseverance are the fuel that powers social media. Invest and the return will be, simply put life altering.

Conclusion

While a powerful marketing tool, social media is not a get rich quick scheme. If an individual is trying to generate awareness of a personality, social media will not garner instant, worldwide notoriety. The success in leveraging social media all lies in having a plan. An individual must be aware of who they are talking to and determine the best way to go about reaching the key audience through a specific channel or channels.

Social media is a dynamic, not a static continuum. What works as far as a strategy at the present time will most likely not work in six months. There needs to be a constant review of strategy to ensure that it continuously aligns with goals and objectives and to ensure strategy continuous to reach the intended.

www.ingramcontent.com/pod-product-compliance
Lightning Source LLC
Chambersburg PA
CBHW071833200526
45169CB00018B/1421